40 Chowder Recipes for Home

By: Kelly Johnson

Table of Contents

- New England Clam Chowder
- Corn Chowder with Bacon
- Potato and Leek Chowder
- Salmon Chowder
- Sweet Potato and Corn Chowder
- Chicken and Corn Chowder
- Roasted Red Pepper and Corn Chowder
- Manhattan Clam Chowder
- Crab and Corn Chowder
- Shrimp and Bacon Chowder
- Lobster Corn Chowder
- Smoky Corn and Potato Chowder
- Vegetable Chowder
- Cheesy Broccoli Chowder
- Roasted Butternut Squash Chowder
- Chicken and Wild Rice Chowder
- Cajun Shrimp and Sausage Chowder
- Spicy Southwest Corn Chowder
- Chipotle Chicken Chowder
- Tomato Basil Chowder
- Thai Coconut Seafood Chowder
- Mushroom and Brie Chowder
- Spinach and Artichoke Chowder
- Italian Sausage and Kale Chowder
- Black Bean and Chorizo Chowder
- Turkey and Sweet Potato Chowder
- White Bean and Escarole Chowder
- Pumpkin and Sage Chowder
- Chicken Tortilla Chowder
- Greek Lemon Chicken Chowder
- Curry Lentil Chowder
- Jalapeño Popper Corn Chowder
- Clam and Bacon Chowder
- Creamy Asparagus and Ham Chowder
- Spinach and White Bean Chowder

- Chicken and Poblano Chowder
- Apple and Cheddar Chowder
- Smoked Salmon Chowder
- Ham and Potato Chowder
- Creamy Cauliflower Chowder

New England Clam Chowder

Ingredients:

- 6 slices bacon, chopped
- 1 onion, finely chopped
- 2 celery stalks, diced
- 3 tablespoons all-purpose flour
- 3 cups potatoes, peeled and diced
- 2 cups chicken broth
- 2 cups clam juice
- 1 bay leaf
- 1 teaspoon dried thyme
- 1/2 teaspoon ground black pepper
- 2 cups heavy cream
- 2 cans (10 ounces each) chopped clams, undrained
- Salt, to taste
- Fresh parsley, chopped, for garnish
- Oyster crackers, for serving (optional)

Instructions:

In a large pot, cook the chopped bacon over medium heat until crispy. Remove some bacon bits for garnish and leave some in the pot for flavor.
Add finely chopped onion and diced celery to the pot. Cook until the vegetables are softened, about 5 minutes.
Sprinkle flour over the vegetables and bacon, stirring constantly, for 2-3 minutes to make a roux.
Add diced potatoes, chicken broth, clam juice, bay leaf, dried thyme, and ground black pepper to the pot. Stir well to combine.
Bring the mixture to a simmer and cook until the potatoes are tender, about 15-20 minutes.
Stir in the heavy cream and chopped clams with their juice. Simmer for an additional 5-10 minutes.
Season the New England Clam Chowder with salt to taste. Keep in mind that clams and bacon are already salty, so adjust accordingly.
Remove the bay leaf from the chowder.
Ladle the chowder into bowls.
Garnish each bowl with the reserved bacon bits and chopped fresh parsley.

Serve hot, optionally with oyster crackers on the side.
Enjoy this classic and hearty New England Clam Chowder!

This rich and creamy clam chowder captures the essence of New England's comfort food tradition.

Corn Chowder with Bacon

Ingredients:

- 6 slices bacon, chopped
- 1 onion, finely chopped
- 2 celery stalks, diced
- 1 red bell pepper, diced
- 3 tablespoons all-purpose flour
- 4 cups frozen corn kernels
- 4 cups chicken broth
- 2 large potatoes, peeled and diced
- 1 bay leaf
- 1 teaspoon dried thyme
- 1/2 teaspoon smoked paprika
- Salt and black pepper to taste
- 2 cups milk
- 1 cup heavy cream
- Fresh chives, chopped, for garnish
- Shredded cheddar cheese, for garnish (optional)

Instructions:

In a large pot, cook the chopped bacon over medium heat until crispy. Remove some bacon bits for garnish and leave some in the pot for flavor.
Add finely chopped onion, diced celery, and diced red bell pepper to the pot. Cook until the vegetables are softened, about 5 minutes.
Sprinkle flour over the vegetables and bacon, stirring constantly, for 2-3 minutes to make a roux.
Add frozen corn kernels, chicken broth, diced potatoes, bay leaf, dried thyme, smoked paprika, salt, and black pepper to the pot. Stir well to combine.
Bring the mixture to a simmer and cook until the potatoes are tender, about 15-20 minutes.
Stir in milk and heavy cream. Simmer for an additional 5-10 minutes, allowing the flavors to meld.
Adjust the seasoning with salt and black pepper if needed.
Remove the bay leaf from the chowder.
Ladle the Corn Chowder with Bacon into bowls.

Garnish each bowl with the reserved bacon bits, chopped fresh chives, and shredded cheddar cheese if desired.
Serve hot and enjoy this creamy and flavorful Corn Chowder with Bacon!

This comforting chowder combines the sweetness of corn with the savory goodness of bacon, creating a delightful bowl of warmth.

Potato and Leek Chowder

Ingredients:

- 4 tablespoons unsalted butter
- 3 leeks, white and light green parts, thinly sliced
- 4 potatoes, peeled and diced
- 1 onion, finely chopped
- 2 cloves garlic, minced
- 4 cups vegetable broth
- 1 bay leaf
- 1 teaspoon dried thyme
- Salt and black pepper to taste
- 2 cups whole milk
- 1 cup heavy cream
- Chives, chopped, for garnish
- Grated cheddar cheese, for garnish (optional)

Instructions:

In a large pot, melt the butter over medium heat. Add the sliced leeks, diced potatoes, finely chopped onion, and minced garlic. Cook until the vegetables are softened, about 5-7 minutes.

Pour in the vegetable broth, add the bay leaf, dried thyme, salt, and black pepper to taste. Stir well to combine.

Bring the mixture to a simmer, then reduce the heat to low, cover, and let it cook until the potatoes are tender, about 15-20 minutes.

Remove the bay leaf from the pot.

Using an immersion blender, blend a portion of the chowder to reach your desired consistency. You can also transfer a portion to a blender and blend, then return it to the pot.

Stir in the whole milk and heavy cream. Simmer for an additional 5-10 minutes to heat through.

Adjust the seasoning with salt and black pepper if needed.

Ladle the Potato and Leek Chowder into bowls.

Garnish each bowl with chopped chives and grated cheddar cheese if desired.

Serve hot and enjoy this comforting Potato and Leek Chowder!

This chowder is rich and creamy, with the mild onion flavor of leeks complementing the hearty potatoes for a satisfying bowl of goodness.

Salmon Chowder

Ingredients:

- 1 pound salmon fillets, skin removed, cut into bite-sized chunks
- 4 slices bacon, chopped
- 1 onion, finely chopped
- 2 celery stalks, diced
- 2 carrots, diced
- 3 potatoes, peeled and diced
- 3 cloves garlic, minced
- 4 cups fish or vegetable broth
- 1 bay leaf
- 1 teaspoon dried thyme
- Salt and black pepper to taste
- 2 cups whole milk
- 1 cup heavy cream
- 2 tablespoons all-purpose flour
- Fresh dill, chopped, for garnish
- Lemon wedges, for serving

Instructions:

In a large pot, cook the chopped bacon over medium heat until crispy. Remove some bacon bits for garnish and leave some in the pot for flavor.
Add finely chopped onion, diced celery, diced carrots, and minced garlic to the pot. Cook until the vegetables are softened, about 5-7 minutes.
Sprinkle flour over the vegetables and bacon, stirring constantly, for 2-3 minutes to make a roux.
Add diced potatoes, salmon chunks, fish or vegetable broth, bay leaf, dried thyme, salt, and black pepper to the pot. Stir well to combine.
Bring the mixture to a simmer and cook until the potatoes are tender and the salmon is cooked through, about 10-15 minutes.
Remove the bay leaf from the pot.
Stir in whole milk and heavy cream. Simmer for an additional 5-10 minutes.
Adjust the seasoning with salt and black pepper if needed.
Ladle the Salmon Chowder into bowls.

Garnish each bowl with the reserved bacon bits, chopped fresh dill, and lemon wedges.
Serve hot and enjoy this rich and flavorful Salmon Chowder!

This chowder combines the richness of salmon with creamy goodness, creating a comforting and satisfying soup.

Sweet Potato and Corn Chowder

Ingredients:

- 2 tablespoons olive oil
- 1 onion, finely chopped
- 2 cloves garlic, minced
- 3 sweet potatoes, peeled and diced
- 3 cups frozen corn kernels
- 4 cups vegetable broth
- 1 bay leaf
- 1 teaspoon ground cumin
- 1 teaspoon smoked paprika
- Salt and black pepper to taste
- 2 cups whole milk
- 1 cup heavy cream
- Fresh cilantro, chopped, for garnish
- Jalapeño slices, for garnish (optional)

Instructions:

In a large pot, heat the olive oil over medium heat. Add the finely chopped onion and cook until softened, about 5 minutes.
Add the minced garlic to the pot and cook for an additional 1-2 minutes until fragrant.
Stir in the diced sweet potatoes and frozen corn kernels. Cook for 5-7 minutes, allowing the vegetables to slightly brown.
Pour in the vegetable broth, add the bay leaf, ground cumin, smoked paprika, salt, and black pepper. Stir well to combine.
Bring the mixture to a simmer, then reduce the heat to low, cover, and let it cook until the sweet potatoes are tender, about 15-20 minutes.
Remove the bay leaf from the pot.
Stir in the whole milk and heavy cream. Simmer for an additional 5-10 minutes to heat through.
Adjust the seasoning with salt and black pepper if needed.
Ladle the Sweet Potato and Corn Chowder into bowls.
Garnish each bowl with chopped fresh cilantro and jalapeño slices if desired.
Serve hot and enjoy this flavorful and hearty Sweet Potato and Corn Chowder!

This chowder combines the natural sweetness of sweet potatoes with the freshness of corn, creating a comforting and nutritious soup.

Chicken and Corn Chowder

Ingredients:

- 2 tablespoons olive oil
- 1 onion, finely chopped
- 2 celery stalks, diced
- 2 carrots, diced
- 3 cloves garlic, minced
- 1 pound boneless, skinless chicken breasts, diced
- 3 tablespoons all-purpose flour
- 4 cups chicken broth
- 2 cups frozen corn kernels
- 1 bay leaf
- 1 teaspoon dried thyme
- Salt and black pepper to taste
- 2 cups whole milk
- 1 cup heavy cream
- Fresh parsley, chopped, for garnish
- Shredded cheddar cheese, for garnish (optional)

Instructions:

In a large pot, heat the olive oil over medium heat. Add the finely chopped onion, diced celery, diced carrots, and minced garlic. Cook until the vegetables are softened, about 5-7 minutes.

Add the diced chicken to the pot and cook until browned on all sides.

Sprinkle the flour over the chicken and vegetables, stirring constantly, for 2-3 minutes to create a roux.

Pour in the chicken broth, add the bay leaf, dried thyme, salt, and black pepper. Stir well to combine.

Bring the mixture to a simmer, then reduce the heat to low, cover, and let it cook until the chicken is cooked through and the vegetables are tender, about 15-20 minutes.

Remove the bay leaf from the pot.

Stir in the frozen corn, whole milk, and heavy cream. Simmer for an additional 5-10 minutes to heat through.

Adjust the seasoning with salt and black pepper if needed.

Ladle the Chicken and Corn Chowder into bowls.
Garnish each bowl with chopped fresh parsley and shredded cheddar cheese if desired.
Serve hot and enjoy this creamy and comforting Chicken and Corn Chowder!

This chowder combines the hearty goodness of chicken with the sweetness of corn for a satisfying and flavorful soup.

Roasted Red Pepper and Corn Chowder

Ingredients:

- 2 tablespoons olive oil
- 1 onion, finely chopped
- 2 cloves garlic, minced
- 2 red bell peppers, roasted and diced
- 3 cups frozen corn kernels
- 4 cups vegetable broth
- 1 bay leaf
- 1 teaspoon smoked paprika
- 1/2 teaspoon cayenne pepper (optional, for heat)
- Salt and black pepper to taste
- 2 cups whole milk
- 1 cup heavy cream
- Fresh cilantro, chopped, for garnish
- Crumbled feta cheese, for garnish (optional)

Instructions:

In a large pot, heat the olive oil over medium heat. Add the finely chopped onion and cook until softened, about 5 minutes.

Add the minced garlic to the pot and cook for an additional 1-2 minutes until fragrant.

Stir in the roasted and diced red bell peppers, frozen corn kernels, vegetable broth, bay leaf, smoked paprika, cayenne pepper (if using), salt, and black pepper. Stir well to combine.

Bring the mixture to a simmer, then reduce the heat to low, cover, and let it cook for about 15-20 minutes.

Remove the bay leaf from the pot.

Stir in the whole milk and heavy cream. Simmer for an additional 5-10 minutes to heat through.

Adjust the seasoning with salt and black pepper if needed.

Ladle the Roasted Red Pepper and Corn Chowder into bowls.

Garnish each bowl with chopped fresh cilantro and crumbled feta cheese if desired.

Serve hot and enjoy this flavorful and vibrant Roasted Red Pepper and Corn Chowder!

This chowder combines the smokiness of roasted red peppers with the sweetness of corn, creating a rich and satisfying soup.

Manhattan Clam Chowder

Ingredients:

- 2 tablespoons olive oil
- 1 onion, finely chopped
- 2 carrots, diced
- 2 celery stalks, diced
- 3 cloves garlic, minced
- 1 bell pepper, diced
- 1 can (28 ounces) crushed tomatoes
- 4 cups vegetable or clam juice
- 2 cups water
- 1 bay leaf
- 1 teaspoon dried thyme
- 1 teaspoon dried oregano
- 1/2 teaspoon red pepper flakes (adjust to taste)
- Salt and black pepper to taste
- 3 cups diced potatoes
- 2 cans (10 ounces each) chopped clams, drained (reserve juice)
- Fresh parsley, chopped, for garnish

Instructions:

In a large pot, heat the olive oil over medium heat. Add the finely chopped onion, diced carrots, diced celery, minced garlic, and diced bell pepper. Cook until the vegetables are softened, about 5-7 minutes.
Add the crushed tomatoes, vegetable or clam juice, water, bay leaf, dried thyme, dried oregano, red pepper flakes, salt, and black pepper. Stir well to combine.
Bring the mixture to a simmer, then reduce the heat to low, cover, and let it cook for about 15-20 minutes.
Add the diced potatoes to the pot and continue to simmer until the potatoes are tender, about 15 minutes.
Stir in the chopped clams and the reserved clam juice. Simmer for an additional 5-10 minutes.
Adjust the seasoning with salt and black pepper if needed.
Remove the bay leaf from the pot.
Ladle the Manhattan Clam Chowder into bowls.

Garnish each bowl with chopped fresh parsley.
Serve hot and enjoy this tangy and savory Manhattan Clam Chowder!

This tomato-based clam chowder is a flavorful and lighter alternative to the creamy New England version, perfect for seafood lovers.

Crab and Corn Chowder

Ingredients:

- 2 tablespoons butter
- 1 onion, finely chopped
- 2 celery stalks, diced
- 2 carrots, diced
- 3 cloves garlic, minced
- 1 red bell pepper, diced
- 3 tablespoons all-purpose flour
- 4 cups chicken or vegetable broth
- 2 cups potatoes, peeled and diced
- 2 cups frozen corn kernels
- 1 bay leaf
- 1 teaspoon dried thyme
- 1/2 teaspoon Old Bay seasoning
- Salt and black pepper to taste
- 2 cups whole milk
- 1 cup heavy cream
- 1 pound lump crabmeat, picked over for shells
- Fresh parsley, chopped, for garnish
- Lemon wedges, for serving

Instructions:

In a large pot, melt the butter over medium heat. Add the finely chopped onion, diced celery, diced carrots, minced garlic, and diced red bell pepper. Cook until the vegetables are softened, about 5-7 minutes.

Sprinkle flour over the vegetables, stirring constantly, for 2-3 minutes to make a roux.

Pour in the chicken or vegetable broth, add the diced potatoes, frozen corn kernels, bay leaf, dried thyme, Old Bay seasoning, salt, and black pepper. Stir well to combine.

Bring the mixture to a simmer, then reduce the heat to low, cover, and let it cook until the potatoes are tender, about 15-20 minutes.

Remove the bay leaf from the pot.

Stir in the whole milk and heavy cream. Simmer for an additional 5-10 minutes.

Adjust the seasoning with salt and black pepper if needed.
Gently fold in the lump crabmeat, being careful not to break up the crab too much. Simmer for an additional 5 minutes until the crab is heated through.
Ladle the Crab and Corn Chowder into bowls.
Garnish each bowl with chopped fresh parsley.
Serve hot, with lemon wedges on the side for squeezing over the chowder.
Enjoy this rich and flavorful Crab and Corn Chowder!

This chowder combines the sweetness of crabmeat with the freshness of corn for a delightful seafood soup.

Shrimp and Bacon Chowder

Ingredients:

- 6 slices bacon, chopped
- 1 onion, finely chopped
- 2 celery stalks, diced
- 2 carrots, diced
- 3 cloves garlic, minced
- 1 red bell pepper, diced
- 3 tablespoons all-purpose flour
- 4 cups chicken or vegetable broth
- 2 cups potatoes, peeled and diced
- 2 cups frozen corn kernels
- 1 bay leaf
- 1 teaspoon dried thyme
- 1/2 teaspoon smoked paprika
- Salt and black pepper to taste
- 2 cups whole milk
- 1 cup heavy cream
- 1 pound medium shrimp, peeled and deveined
- Fresh parsley, chopped, for garnish
- Green onions, sliced, for garnish

Instructions:

In a large pot, cook the chopped bacon over medium heat until crispy. Remove some bacon bits for garnish and leave some in the pot for flavor.
Add the finely chopped onion, diced celery, diced carrots, minced garlic, and diced red bell pepper to the pot. Cook until the vegetables are softened, about 5-7 minutes.
Sprinkle flour over the vegetables and bacon, stirring constantly, for 2-3 minutes to make a roux.
Pour in the chicken or vegetable broth, add the diced potatoes, frozen corn kernels, bay leaf, dried thyme, smoked paprika, salt, and black pepper. Stir well to combine.
Bring the mixture to a simmer, then reduce the heat to low, cover, and let it cook until the potatoes are tender, about 15-20 minutes.
Remove the bay leaf from the pot.

Stir in the whole milk and heavy cream. Simmer for an additional 5-10 minutes.
Adjust the seasoning with salt and black pepper if needed.
Gently fold in the peeled and deveined shrimp. Cook for an additional 5-7 minutes until the shrimp are pink and cooked through.
Ladle the Shrimp and Bacon Chowder into bowls.
Garnish each bowl with the reserved bacon bits, chopped fresh parsley, and sliced green onions.
Serve hot and enjoy this rich and flavorful Shrimp and Bacon Chowder!

This chowder combines the savory goodness of bacon with the succulence of shrimp for a hearty and satisfying soup.

Lobster Corn Chowder

Ingredients:

- 2 lobster tails, shells removed and meat diced
- 4 tablespoons unsalted butter
- 1 onion, finely chopped
- 2 celery stalks, diced
- 2 carrots, diced
- 3 cloves garlic, minced
- 3 tablespoons all-purpose flour
- 4 cups seafood or vegetable broth
- 2 cups potatoes, peeled and diced
- 2 cups frozen corn kernels
- 1 bay leaf
- 1 teaspoon dried thyme
- 1/2 teaspoon Old Bay seasoning
- Salt and black pepper to taste
- 2 cups whole milk
- 1 cup heavy cream
- Fresh parsley, chopped, for garnish
- Chives, chopped, for garnish (optional)

Instructions:

In a large pot, melt 2 tablespoons of butter over medium heat. Add the diced lobster meat and sauté until cooked through. Remove the lobster from the pot and set aside.
In the same pot, add the remaining 2 tablespoons of butter. Add the finely chopped onion, diced celery, diced carrots, and minced garlic. Cook until the vegetables are softened, about 5-7 minutes.
Sprinkle flour over the vegetables, stirring constantly, for 2-3 minutes to make a roux.
Pour in the seafood or vegetable broth, add the diced potatoes, frozen corn kernels, bay leaf, dried thyme, Old Bay seasoning, salt, and black pepper. Stir well to combine.
Bring the mixture to a simmer, then reduce the heat to low, cover, and let it cook until the potatoes are tender, about 15-20 minutes.

Remove the bay leaf from the pot.
Stir in the whole milk and heavy cream. Simmer for an additional 5-10 minutes.
Adjust the seasoning with salt and black pepper if needed.
Gently fold in the sautéed lobster meat.
Ladle the Lobster Corn Chowder into bowls.
Garnish each bowl with chopped fresh parsley and chives if desired.
Serve hot and enjoy this decadent Lobster Corn Chowder!

This chowder combines the sweet and delicate flavor of lobster with the sweetness of corn for a luxurious and delightful soup.

Smoky Corn and Potato Chowder

Ingredients:

- 2 tablespoons olive oil
- 1 onion, finely chopped
- 2 cloves garlic, minced
- 2 celery stalks, diced
- 2 carrots, diced
- 3 cups potatoes, peeled and diced
- 4 cups frozen corn kernels
- 6 cups vegetable or chicken broth
- 1 teaspoon smoked paprika
- 1/2 teaspoon cumin
- 1 bay leaf
- Salt and black pepper to taste
- 2 cups whole milk
- 1 cup heavy cream
- 1 cup shredded smoked gouda cheese
- Fresh chives, chopped, for garnish

Instructions:

In a large pot, heat the olive oil over medium heat. Add the finely chopped onion, minced garlic, diced celery, and diced carrots. Cook until the vegetables are softened, about 5-7 minutes.

Add the diced potatoes and frozen corn to the pot. Stir well to combine.

Pour in the vegetable or chicken broth, add the smoked paprika, cumin, bay leaf, salt, and black pepper. Stir to combine.

Bring the mixture to a simmer, then reduce the heat to low, cover, and let it cook until the potatoes are tender, about 15-20 minutes.

Remove the bay leaf from the pot.

Stir in the whole milk and heavy cream. Simmer for an additional 5-10 minutes.

Gently fold in the shredded smoked gouda cheese until melted and well combined.

Adjust the seasoning with salt and black pepper if needed.

Ladle the Smoky Corn and Potato Chowder into bowls.

Garnish each bowl with chopped fresh chives.

Serve hot and enjoy this flavorful and smoky Corn and Potato Chowder!

This chowder features the smoky flavor of paprika and gouda cheese, creating a rich and comforting soup with a delightful depth of taste.

Vegetable Chowder

Ingredients:

- 2 tablespoons olive oil
- 1 onion, finely chopped
- 2 cloves garlic, minced
- 2 carrots, diced
- 2 celery stalks, diced
- 1 bell pepper, diced (any color)
- 3 cups potatoes, peeled and diced
- 4 cups vegetable broth
- 1 bay leaf
- 1 teaspoon dried thyme
- 1/2 teaspoon smoked paprika
- Salt and black pepper to taste
- 2 cups frozen corn kernels
- 1 cup green beans, trimmed and chopped
- 2 cups whole milk
- 1 cup heavy cream
- Fresh parsley, chopped, for garnish

Instructions:

In a large pot, heat the olive oil over medium heat. Add the finely chopped onion, minced garlic, diced carrots, diced celery, and diced bell pepper. Cook until the vegetables are softened, about 5-7 minutes.
Add the diced potatoes to the pot. Stir well to combine.
Pour in the vegetable broth, add the bay leaf, dried thyme, smoked paprika, salt, and black pepper. Stir to combine.
Bring the mixture to a simmer, then reduce the heat to low, cover, and let it cook until the potatoes are tender, about 15-20 minutes.
Remove the bay leaf from the pot.
Stir in the frozen corn and chopped green beans. Simmer for an additional 5-7 minutes.
Stir in the whole milk and heavy cream. Simmer for an additional 5-10 minutes.
Adjust the seasoning with salt and black pepper if needed.
Ladle the Vegetable Chowder into bowls.
Garnish each bowl with chopped fresh parsley.

Serve hot and enjoy this nutritious and flavorful Vegetable Chowder!

This chowder is packed with a variety of colorful vegetables, creating a satisfying and comforting soup that's perfect for any season.

Cheesy Broccoli Chowder

Ingredients:

- 2 tablespoons butter
- 1 onion, finely chopped
- 2 cloves garlic, minced
- 3 tablespoons all-purpose flour
- 4 cups vegetable or chicken broth
- 3 cups broccoli florets, chopped
- 2 carrots, grated
- 2 cups potatoes, peeled and diced
- 1 bay leaf
- 1 teaspoon dried thyme
- Salt and black pepper to taste
- 2 cups whole milk
- 1 cup heavy cream
- 2 cups shredded sharp cheddar cheese
- Fresh parsley, chopped, for garnish

Instructions:

In a large pot, melt the butter over medium heat. Add the finely chopped onion and minced garlic. Cook until the onion is softened, about 5 minutes.
Sprinkle flour over the onions and garlic, stirring constantly, for 2-3 minutes to make a roux.
Pour in the vegetable or chicken broth, stirring continuously to avoid lumps.
Add the chopped broccoli, grated carrots, diced potatoes, bay leaf, dried thyme, salt, and black pepper. Stir well to combine.
Bring the mixture to a simmer, then reduce the heat to low, cover, and let it cook until the vegetables are tender, about 15-20 minutes.
Remove the bay leaf from the pot.
Stir in the whole milk and heavy cream. Simmer for an additional 5-10 minutes.
Gently fold in the shredded sharp cheddar cheese until melted and well combined.
Adjust the seasoning with salt and black pepper if needed.
Ladle the Cheesy Broccoli Chowder into bowls.
Garnish each bowl with chopped fresh parsley.

Serve hot and enjoy this creamy and cheesy Broccoli Chowder!

This chowder combines the richness of cheddar cheese with the goodness of broccoli, creating a comforting and flavorful soup.

Roasted Butternut Squash Chowder

Ingredients:

- 1 medium-sized butternut squash, peeled, seeded, and diced
- 2 tablespoons olive oil
- Salt and black pepper to taste
- 4 tablespoons butter
- 1 onion, finely chopped
- 2 cloves garlic, minced
- 3 tablespoons all-purpose flour
- 4 cups vegetable or chicken broth
- 2 carrots, diced
- 2 celery stalks, diced
- 1 bay leaf
- 1 teaspoon dried thyme
- 1/2 teaspoon ground nutmeg
- 2 cups whole milk
- 1 cup heavy cream
- Fresh parsley, chopped, for garnish
- Croutons or toasted pumpkin seeds, for topping (optional)

Instructions:

Preheat the oven to 400°F (200°C).
Toss the diced butternut squash with olive oil, salt, and black pepper. Place it on a baking sheet in a single layer. Roast in the preheated oven for about 25-30 minutes or until the squash is tender and slightly caramelized. Set aside.
In a large pot, melt the butter over medium heat. Add the finely chopped onion and cook until softened, about 5 minutes.
Add the minced garlic and cook for an additional 1-2 minutes until fragrant.
Sprinkle flour over the onions and garlic, stirring constantly, for 2-3 minutes to make a roux.
Pour in the vegetable or chicken broth, stirring continuously to avoid lumps.
Add the diced carrots, diced celery, bay leaf, dried thyme, and ground nutmeg. Stir well to combine.
Bring the mixture to a simmer, then reduce the heat to low, cover, and let it cook until the vegetables are tender, about 15-20 minutes.
Remove the bay leaf from the pot.

Stir in the roasted butternut squash.
Add the whole milk and heavy cream. Simmer for an additional 5-10 minutes.
Adjust the seasoning with salt and black pepper if needed.
Ladle the Roasted Butternut Squash Chowder into bowls.
Garnish each bowl with chopped fresh parsley.
Optionally, top with croutons or toasted pumpkin seeds for added texture.
Serve hot and enjoy this creamy and comforting Roasted Butternut Squash Chowder!

This chowder highlights the sweet and nutty flavor of roasted butternut squash, creating a rich and satisfying soup.

Chicken and Wild Rice Chowder

Ingredients:

- 1 cup wild rice, uncooked
- 4 cups chicken broth
- 2 tablespoons olive oil
- 1 onion, finely chopped
- 2 carrots, diced
- 2 celery stalks, diced
- 3 cloves garlic, minced
- 1 teaspoon dried thyme
- 1/2 teaspoon dried rosemary
- 1 bay leaf
- Salt and black pepper to taste
- 1 rotisserie chicken, shredded (about 3 cups)
- 1/2 cup all-purpose flour
- 4 cups whole milk
- 1 cup heavy cream
- Fresh parsley, chopped, for garnish

Instructions:

Cook the wild rice according to package instructions, using chicken broth instead of water. Set aside.

In a large pot, heat the olive oil over medium heat. Add the finely chopped onion, diced carrots, and diced celery. Cook until the vegetables are softened, about 5-7 minutes.

Add the minced garlic, dried thyme, dried rosemary, bay leaf, salt, and black pepper. Stir well to combine.

Stir in the shredded rotisserie chicken and cooked wild rice.

Sprinkle flour over the chicken and rice mixture, stirring constantly, for 2-3 minutes to make a roux.

Pour in the whole milk and heavy cream, stirring continuously to avoid lumps.

Bring the mixture to a simmer, then reduce the heat to low, cover, and let it cook for about 15-20 minutes.

Remove the bay leaf from the pot.

Adjust the seasoning with salt and black pepper if needed.

Ladle the Chicken and Wild Rice Chowder into bowls.
Garnish each bowl with chopped fresh parsley.
Serve hot and enjoy this hearty and comforting Chicken and Wild Rice Chowder!

This chowder combines the earthy flavor of wild rice with the comforting taste of shredded chicken, creating a satisfying and flavorful soup.

Cajun Shrimp and Sausage Chowder

Ingredients:

- 1 pound large shrimp, peeled and deveined
- 8 ounces Andouille sausage, sliced
- 2 tablespoons olive oil
- 1 onion, finely chopped
- 2 bell peppers (any color), diced
- 3 celery stalks, diced
- 3 cloves garlic, minced
- 1 teaspoon Cajun seasoning (adjust to taste)
- 1/2 teaspoon smoked paprika
- 1/2 teaspoon dried thyme
- 1 bay leaf
- Salt and black pepper to taste
- 1/4 cup all-purpose flour
- 4 cups chicken broth
- 1 cup whole milk
- 1 cup heavy cream
- 2 cups frozen corn kernels
- 1 cup okra, sliced (fresh or frozen)
- Cooked rice, for serving
- Green onions, sliced, for garnish

Instructions:

In a large pot, heat the olive oil over medium heat. Add the sliced Andouille sausage and cook until browned. Remove the sausage and set aside.
In the same pot, add the finely chopped onion, diced bell peppers, and diced celery. Cook until the vegetables are softened, about 5-7 minutes.
Add the minced garlic, Cajun seasoning, smoked paprika, dried thyme, bay leaf, salt, and black pepper. Stir well to combine.
Sprinkle flour over the vegetables, stirring constantly, for 2-3 minutes to make a roux.
Pour in the chicken broth, stirring continuously to avoid lumps.
Add the cooked Andouille sausage back to the pot.
Bring the mixture to a simmer, then reduce the heat to low, cover, and let it cook for about 15-20 minutes.

Add the whole milk, heavy cream, frozen corn kernels, and sliced okra. Simmer for an additional 5-10 minutes.
Adjust the seasoning with salt, black pepper, and Cajun seasoning if needed.
Add the peeled and deveined shrimp to the pot, and cook until the shrimp are pink and cooked through.
Remove the bay leaf from the pot.
Serve the Cajun Shrimp and Sausage Chowder over cooked rice.
Garnish with sliced green onions.
Enjoy this spicy and hearty Cajun-inspired chowder!

This chowder combines the bold flavors of Cajun seasoning with shrimp, sausage, and a mix of vegetables for a delicious and satisfying soup.

Spicy Southwest Corn Chowder

Ingredients:

- 2 tablespoons olive oil
- 1 onion, finely chopped
- 2 bell peppers (red and/or green), diced
- 2 jalapeño peppers, seeded and finely chopped
- 3 cloves garlic, minced
- 1 teaspoon ground cumin
- 1 teaspoon chili powder
- 1/2 teaspoon smoked paprika
- 1/2 teaspoon cayenne pepper (adjust to taste)
- 4 cups frozen corn kernels
- 4 cups vegetable or chicken broth
- 2 cups potatoes, peeled and diced
- 1 can (14 ounces) diced tomatoes, undrained
- 1 bay leaf
- Salt and black pepper to taste
- 1 cup whole milk
- 1 cup heavy cream
- Fresh cilantro, chopped, for garnish
- Avocado slices, for garnish (optional)
- Lime wedges, for serving

Instructions:

In a large pot, heat the olive oil over medium heat. Add the finely chopped onion, diced bell peppers, and chopped jalapeño peppers. Cook until the vegetables are softened, about 5-7 minutes.

Add the minced garlic, ground cumin, chili powder, smoked paprika, and cayenne pepper. Stir well to combine.

Add the frozen corn, vegetable or chicken broth, diced potatoes, diced tomatoes (with their juice), and bay leaf. Stir well.

Season with salt and black pepper to taste. Bring the mixture to a simmer, then reduce the heat to low, cover, and let it cook until the potatoes are tender, about 15-20 minutes.

Remove the bay leaf from the pot.

Stir in the whole milk and heavy cream. Simmer for an additional 5-10 minutes.

Adjust the seasoning with salt and black pepper if needed.
Ladle the Spicy Southwest Corn Chowder into bowls.
Garnish each bowl with chopped fresh cilantro and, if desired, avocado slices.
Serve hot with lime wedges on the side for squeezing over the chowder.
Enjoy this Spicy Southwest Corn Chowder with a kick of heat and a blend of vibrant flavors!

This chowder brings together the bold and spicy elements of Southwest cuisine with the sweetness of corn for a soup that's both hearty and full of flavor.

Chipotle Chicken Chowder

Ingredients:

- 2 tablespoons olive oil
- 1 onion, finely chopped
- 2 bell peppers (red and/or green), diced
- 3 cloves garlic, minced
- 1 teaspoon ground cumin
- 1 teaspoon chili powder
- 1/2 teaspoon smoked paprika
- 1/2 teaspoon dried oregano
- 2 chipotle peppers in adobo sauce, minced
- 1 can (14 ounces) diced tomatoes, undrained
- 4 cups chicken broth
- 2 cups cooked chicken, shredded
- 2 cups frozen corn kernels
- 1 cup potatoes, peeled and diced
- 1 cup whole milk
- 1 cup heavy cream
- Salt and black pepper to taste
- Fresh cilantro, chopped, for garnish
- Lime wedges, for serving

Instructions:

In a large pot, heat the olive oil over medium heat. Add the finely chopped onion and diced bell peppers. Cook until the vegetables are softened, about 5-7 minutes.
Add the minced garlic, ground cumin, chili powder, smoked paprika, dried oregano, and minced chipotle peppers. Stir well to combine.
Add the diced tomatoes (with their juice), chicken broth, shredded chicken, frozen corn, and diced potatoes. Stir well.
Bring the mixture to a simmer, then reduce the heat to low, cover, and let it cook until the potatoes are tender, about 15-20 minutes.
Stir in the whole milk and heavy cream. Simmer for an additional 5-10 minutes.
Adjust the seasoning with salt and black pepper if needed.
Ladle the Chipotle Chicken Chowder into bowls.

Garnish each bowl with chopped fresh cilantro.
Serve hot with lime wedges on the side for squeezing over the chowder.
Enjoy this Chipotle Chicken Chowder with a smoky and spicy kick!

This chowder incorporates the bold and smoky flavor of chipotle peppers, adding a delightful heat to the creamy and comforting chicken soup.

Tomato Basil Chowder

Ingredients:

- 2 tablespoons olive oil
- 1 onion, finely chopped
- 2 carrots, diced
- 2 celery stalks, diced
- 3 cloves garlic, minced
- 1/4 cup all-purpose flour
- 4 cups vegetable or chicken broth
- 1 can (28 ounces) crushed tomatoes
- 1 can (14 ounces) diced tomatoes, undrained
- 1 teaspoon dried basil
- 1/2 teaspoon dried oregano
- 1 bay leaf
- Salt and black pepper to taste
- 1 cup whole milk
- 1/2 cup heavy cream
- Fresh basil, chopped, for garnish
- Grated Parmesan cheese, for serving (optional)

Instructions:

In a large pot, heat the olive oil over medium heat. Add the finely chopped onion, diced carrots, and diced celery. Cook until the vegetables are softened, about 5-7 minutes.
Add the minced garlic and cook for an additional 1-2 minutes until fragrant.
Sprinkle flour over the vegetables, stirring constantly, for 2-3 minutes to make a roux.
Pour in the vegetable or chicken broth, crushed tomatoes, diced tomatoes (with their juice), dried basil, dried oregano, bay leaf, salt, and black pepper. Stir well to combine.
Bring the mixture to a simmer, then reduce the heat to low, cover, and let it cook for about 15-20 minutes.
Remove the bay leaf from the pot.
Stir in the whole milk and heavy cream. Simmer for an additional 5-10 minutes.
Adjust the seasoning with salt and black pepper if needed.

Ladle the Tomato Basil Chowder into bowls.
Garnish each bowl with chopped fresh basil.
Optionally, sprinkle grated Parmesan cheese on top.
Serve hot and enjoy this comforting and flavorful Tomato Basil Chowder!

This chowder combines the classic combination of tomatoes and basil for a rich and satisfying soup that's perfect for any time of the year.

Thai Coconut Seafood Chowder

Ingredients:

- 2 tablespoons vegetable oil
- 1 onion, finely chopped
- 2 cloves garlic, minced
- 1 tablespoon ginger, grated
- 2 tablespoons Thai red curry paste
- 1 can (14 ounces) coconut milk
- 4 cups seafood or chicken broth
- 1 lemongrass stalk, bruised
- 2 kaffir lime leaves
- 1 tablespoon fish sauce
- 1 teaspoon sugar
- 1 pound mixed seafood (shrimp, scallops, mussels, etc.)
- 1 red bell pepper, thinly sliced
- 1 cup cherry tomatoes, halved
- 1 cup baby spinach leaves
- Juice of 1 lime
- Fresh cilantro, chopped, for garnish
- Red chili flakes, for garnish (optional)

Instructions:

In a large pot, heat the vegetable oil over medium heat. Add the finely chopped onion and cook until softened, about 5 minutes.
Add the minced garlic and grated ginger. Cook for an additional 2 minutes until fragrant.
Stir in the Thai red curry paste and cook for 1-2 minutes.
Pour in the coconut milk and seafood or chicken broth. Add the bruised lemongrass stalk, kaffir lime leaves, fish sauce, and sugar. Stir well.
Bring the mixture to a gentle simmer, then reduce the heat to low, cover, and let it simmer for about 15-20 minutes to infuse the flavors.
Add the mixed seafood, sliced red bell pepper, and halved cherry tomatoes. Cook until the seafood is cooked through, about 5-7 minutes.
Stir in the baby spinach leaves and lime juice. Cook for an additional 2 minutes until the spinach wilts.
Remove the lemongrass stalk and kaffir lime leaves from the pot.

Adjust the seasoning with fish sauce or lime juice if needed.
Ladle the Thai Coconut Seafood Chowder into bowls.
Garnish each bowl with chopped fresh cilantro and, if desired, red chili flakes for extra heat.
Serve hot and enjoy this flavorful and aromatic Thai Coconut Seafood Chowder!

This chowder combines the richness of coconut milk with the bold flavors of Thai red curry paste and a medley of seafood, creating a delightful and comforting soup.

Mushroom and Brie Chowder

Ingredients:

- 2 tablespoons unsalted butter
- 1 onion, finely chopped
- 2 cloves garlic, minced
- 1 pound mushrooms, sliced
- 1/4 cup all-purpose flour
- 4 cups vegetable or chicken broth
- 2 cups potatoes, peeled and diced
- 1 bay leaf
- 1 teaspoon dried thyme
- Salt and black pepper to taste
- 1 cup whole milk
- 1 cup heavy cream
- 8 ounces Brie cheese, rind removed, and diced
- Fresh chives, chopped, for garnish

Instructions:

In a large pot, melt the butter over medium heat. Add the finely chopped onion and cook until softened, about 5 minutes.
Add the minced garlic and sliced mushrooms. Cook until the mushrooms are browned and have released their moisture, about 8-10 minutes.
Sprinkle flour over the mushrooms, stirring constantly, for 2-3 minutes to make a roux.
Pour in the vegetable or chicken broth, stirring continuously to avoid lumps.
Add the diced potatoes, bay leaf, dried thyme, salt, and black pepper. Stir well to combine.
Bring the mixture to a simmer, then reduce the heat to low, cover, and let it cook until the potatoes are tender, about 15-20 minutes.
Remove the bay leaf from the pot.
Stir in the whole milk and heavy cream. Simmer for an additional 5-10 minutes.
Gently fold in the diced Brie cheese until melted and well combined.
Adjust the seasoning with salt and black pepper if needed.
Ladle the Mushroom and Brie Chowder into bowls.
Garnish each bowl with chopped fresh chives.
Serve hot and enjoy this creamy and luxurious Mushroom and Brie Chowder!

This chowder combines the earthy flavor of mushrooms with the richness of Brie cheese, creating a velvety and indulgent soup that's perfect for a cozy meal.

Spinach and Artichoke Chowder

Ingredients:

- 2 tablespoons unsalted butter
- 1 onion, finely chopped
- 2 cloves garlic, minced
- 1/4 cup all-purpose flour
- 4 cups vegetable or chicken broth
- 2 cups potatoes, peeled and diced
- 1 bay leaf
- 1 teaspoon dried thyme
- Salt and black pepper to taste
- 1 cup whole milk
- 1 cup heavy cream
- 1 can (14 ounces) artichoke hearts, drained and chopped
- 2 cups fresh baby spinach leaves
- 1 cup shredded Parmesan cheese
- Fresh parsley, chopped, for garnish

Instructions:

In a large pot, melt the butter over medium heat. Add the finely chopped onion and cook until softened, about 5 minutes.
Add the minced garlic and cook for an additional 1-2 minutes until fragrant.
Sprinkle flour over the onions and garlic, stirring constantly, for 2-3 minutes to make a roux.
Pour in the vegetable or chicken broth, stirring continuously to avoid lumps.
Add the diced potatoes, bay leaf, dried thyme, salt, and black pepper. Stir well to combine.
Bring the mixture to a simmer, then reduce the heat to low, cover, and let it cook until the potatoes are tender, about 15-20 minutes.
Remove the bay leaf from the pot.
Stir in the whole milk and heavy cream. Simmer for an additional 5-10 minutes.
Gently fold in the chopped artichoke hearts, fresh baby spinach, and shredded Parmesan cheese until well combined.
Adjust the seasoning with salt and black pepper if needed.
Ladle the Spinach and Artichoke Chowder into bowls.

Garnish each bowl with chopped fresh parsley.
Serve hot and enjoy this creamy and flavorful Spinach and Artichoke Chowder!

This chowder combines the classic flavors of spinach and artichoke dip into a comforting soup that's both rich and satisfying.

Italian Sausage and Kale Chowder

Ingredients:

- 1 pound Italian sausage, casings removed
- 2 tablespoons olive oil
- 1 onion, finely chopped
- 3 cloves garlic, minced
- 2 carrots, diced
- 2 celery stalks, diced
- 1 teaspoon dried oregano
- 1 teaspoon dried thyme
- 1/2 teaspoon red pepper flakes (optional, for heat)
- 4 cups chicken broth
- 2 cups potatoes, peeled and diced
- 1 bay leaf
- Salt and black pepper to taste
- 1 bunch kale, stems removed and leaves chopped
- 1 cup whole milk
- 1 cup heavy cream
- Grated Parmesan cheese, for serving
- Fresh parsley, chopped, for garnish

Instructions:

In a large pot, cook the Italian sausage over medium heat, breaking it into crumbles, until browned and cooked through. Remove excess fat, if any.

In the same pot, add olive oil and heat over medium heat. Add the finely chopped onion, minced garlic, diced carrots, and diced celery. Cook until the vegetables are softened, about 5-7 minutes.

Stir in the dried oregano, dried thyme, and red pepper flakes (if using).

Pour in the chicken broth, diced potatoes, bay leaf, salt, and black pepper. Stir well to combine.

Bring the mixture to a simmer, then reduce the heat to low, cover, and let it cook until the potatoes are tender, about 15-20 minutes.

Remove the bay leaf from the pot.

Add the chopped kale to the pot and cook until wilted, about 3-5 minutes.

Stir in the whole milk and heavy cream. Simmer for an additional 5-10 minutes.

Adjust the seasoning with salt and black pepper if needed.
Ladle the Italian Sausage and Kale Chowder into bowls.
Serve hot, garnished with grated Parmesan cheese and chopped fresh parsley.
Enjoy this hearty and flavorful Italian Sausage and Kale Chowder!

This chowder combines the robust flavors of Italian sausage with nutritious kale, creating a comforting and satisfying soup.

Black Bean and Chorizo Chowder

Ingredients:

- 1 tablespoon olive oil
- 1 onion, finely chopped
- 3 cloves garlic, minced
- 1 pound chorizo sausage, casing removed and crumbled
- 2 potatoes, peeled and diced
- 2 carrots, diced
- 2 celery stalks, diced
- 2 teaspoons ground cumin
- 1 teaspoon chili powder
- 1/2 teaspoon smoked paprika
- 4 cups chicken broth
- 2 cans (15 ounces each) black beans, drained and rinsed
- 1 cup corn kernels (fresh or frozen)
- 1 bay leaf
- Salt and black pepper to taste
- 1 cup whole milk
- 1 cup heavy cream
- Fresh cilantro, chopped, for garnish
- Lime wedges, for serving

Instructions:

In a large pot, heat olive oil over medium heat. Add the finely chopped onion and cook until softened, about 5 minutes.

Add minced garlic and crumbled chorizo sausage. Cook until the chorizo is browned and cooked through.

Stir in diced potatoes, carrots, and celery. Cook for an additional 5-7 minutes until the vegetables start to soften.

Add ground cumin, chili powder, and smoked paprika. Stir well to coat the ingredients.

Pour in chicken broth, black beans, corn, and add the bay leaf. Season with salt and black pepper to taste.

Bring the mixture to a simmer, then reduce the heat to low, cover, and let it cook until the potatoes and carrots are tender, about 15-20 minutes.

Remove the bay leaf from the pot.

Stir in whole milk and heavy cream. Simmer for an additional 5-10 minutes.
Adjust the seasoning with salt and black pepper if needed.
Ladle the Black Bean and Chorizo Chowder into bowls.
Garnish each bowl with chopped fresh cilantro.
Serve hot with lime wedges on the side for squeezing over the chowder.
Enjoy this flavorful and hearty Black Bean and Chorizo Chowder!

This chowder combines the smoky and spicy flavors of chorizo with black beans and vegetables, creating a robust and satisfying soup.

Turkey and Sweet Potato Chowder

Ingredients:

- 1 tablespoon olive oil
- 1 onion, finely chopped
- 2 cloves garlic, minced
- 1 pound ground turkey
- 2 sweet potatoes, peeled and diced
- 2 carrots, diced
- 2 celery stalks, diced
- 1 teaspoon dried thyme
- 1 teaspoon dried sage
- 4 cups chicken or vegetable broth
- 1 bay leaf
- Salt and black pepper to taste
- 1 cup whole milk
- 1 cup heavy cream
- 1 cup corn kernels (fresh or frozen)
- Fresh parsley, chopped, for garnish

Instructions:

In a large pot, heat olive oil over medium heat. Add the finely chopped onion and cook until softened, about 5 minutes.
Add minced garlic and ground turkey. Cook until the turkey is browned and cooked through.
Stir in diced sweet potatoes, carrots, and celery. Cook for an additional 5-7 minutes until the vegetables start to soften.
Add dried thyme, dried sage, chicken or vegetable broth, and the bay leaf. Season with salt and black pepper to taste.
Bring the mixture to a simmer, then reduce the heat to low, cover, and let it cook until the sweet potatoes and carrots are tender, about 15-20 minutes.
Remove the bay leaf from the pot.
Stir in whole milk and heavy cream. Simmer for an additional 5-10 minutes.
Add corn kernels and cook for an additional 5 minutes.
Adjust the seasoning with salt and black pepper if needed.
Ladle the Turkey and Sweet Potato Chowder into bowls.
Garnish each bowl with chopped fresh parsley.

Serve hot and enjoy this comforting and flavorful Turkey and Sweet Potato Chowder!

This chowder combines the lean protein of ground turkey with the sweetness of sweet potatoes, creating a hearty and nutritious soup.

White Bean and Escarole Chowder

Ingredients:

- 2 tablespoons olive oil
- 1 onion, finely chopped
- 3 cloves garlic, minced
- 1 pound escarole, chopped
- 2 cans (15 ounces each) cannellini beans, drained and rinsed
- 4 cups vegetable or chicken broth
- 2 potatoes, peeled and diced
- 1 bay leaf
- 1 teaspoon dried rosemary
- Salt and black pepper to taste
- 1 cup whole milk
- 1 cup heavy cream
- Grated Parmesan cheese, for serving
- Fresh parsley, chopped, for garnish

Instructions:

In a large pot, heat olive oil over medium heat. Add the finely chopped onion and cook until softened, about 5 minutes.
Add minced garlic and chopped escarole. Cook until the escarole is wilted.
Stir in cannellini beans, vegetable or chicken broth, diced potatoes, bay leaf, dried rosemary, salt, and black pepper. Stir well to combine.
Bring the mixture to a simmer, then reduce the heat to low, cover, and let it cook until the potatoes are tender, about 15-20 minutes.
Remove the bay leaf from the pot.
Stir in whole milk and heavy cream. Simmer for an additional 5-10 minutes.
Adjust the seasoning with salt and black pepper if needed.
Ladle the White Bean and Escarole Chowder into bowls.
Garnish each bowl with grated Parmesan cheese and chopped fresh parsley.
Serve hot and enjoy this nutritious and flavorful White Bean and Escarole Chowder!

This chowder combines the creaminess of white beans with the slightly bitter flavor of escarole, creating a wholesome and satisfying soup.

Pumpkin and Sage Chowder

Ingredients:

- 2 tablespoons unsalted butter
- 1 onion, finely chopped
- 2 cloves garlic, minced
- 1 tablespoon fresh sage leaves, chopped (plus extra for garnish)
- 1/4 cup all-purpose flour
- 4 cups vegetable or chicken broth
- 1 can (15 ounces) pumpkin puree
- 2 potatoes, peeled and diced
- 1 cup carrots, diced
- 1 bay leaf
- 1 teaspoon dried thyme
- Salt and black pepper to taste
- 1 cup whole milk
- 1 cup heavy cream
- Nutmeg, for garnish (optional)
- Pumpkin seeds, toasted, for garnish (optional)

Instructions:

In a large pot, melt the butter over medium heat. Add the finely chopped onion and cook until softened, about 5 minutes.

Add minced garlic and chopped fresh sage leaves. Cook for an additional 1-2 minutes until fragrant.

Sprinkle flour over the onion and sage mixture, stirring constantly, for 2-3 minutes to make a roux.

Pour in the vegetable or chicken broth, stirring continuously to avoid lumps.

Add pumpkin puree, diced potatoes, diced carrots, bay leaf, dried thyme, salt, and black pepper. Stir well to combine.

Bring the mixture to a simmer, then reduce the heat to low, cover, and let it cook until the potatoes and carrots are tender, about 15-20 minutes.

Remove the bay leaf from the pot.

Stir in whole milk and heavy cream. Simmer for an additional 5-10 minutes.

Adjust the seasoning with salt and black pepper if needed.

Ladle the Pumpkin and Sage Chowder into bowls.

Garnish each bowl with additional chopped fresh sage leaves.
Optionally, sprinkle a pinch of nutmeg on top and add toasted pumpkin seeds for extra texture.
Serve hot and enjoy this creamy and comforting Pumpkin and Sage Chowder!

This chowder combines the autumnal flavors of pumpkin and sage for a warm and satisfying soup perfect for fall or any cozy occasion.

Chicken Tortilla Chowder

Ingredients:

- 1 tablespoon vegetable oil
- 1 onion, finely chopped
- 2 cloves garlic, minced
- 1 jalapeño, seeded and finely chopped (optional for heat)
- 1 teaspoon ground cumin
- 1 teaspoon chili powder
- 1 teaspoon dried oregano
- 1 can (14 ounces) diced tomatoes, undrained
- 1 can (4 ounces) chopped green chilies
- 4 cups chicken broth
- 1 pound boneless, skinless chicken breasts, cooked and shredded
- 1 cup corn kernels (fresh or frozen)
- 1 cup black beans, drained and rinsed
- Salt and black pepper to taste
- 1 cup whole milk
- 1 cup shredded cheddar cheese
- 1 cup tortilla strips or chips, for garnish
- Fresh cilantro, chopped, for garnish
- Lime wedges, for serving

Instructions:

In a large pot, heat the vegetable oil over medium heat. Add the finely chopped onion and cook until softened, about 5 minutes.
Add minced garlic and chopped jalapeño (if using). Cook for an additional 1-2 minutes until fragrant.
Stir in ground cumin, chili powder, and dried oregano.
Add diced tomatoes, chopped green chilies, and chicken broth. Bring the mixture to a simmer.
Stir in shredded chicken, corn, and black beans. Season with salt and black pepper to taste.
Simmer the chowder for about 15-20 minutes to allow the flavors to meld.
Stir in whole milk and shredded cheddar cheese. Cook until the cheese is melted and the chowder is heated through.
Adjust the seasoning if needed.

Ladle the Chicken Tortilla Chowder into bowls.
Garnish each bowl with tortilla strips or chips, chopped fresh cilantro, and serve with lime wedges on the side.
Enjoy this delicious and hearty Chicken Tortilla Chowder!

This chowder combines the bold flavors of Mexican spices, shredded chicken, and crunchy tortilla strips for a comforting and satisfying soup.

Greek Lemon Chicken Chowder

Ingredients:

- 1 tablespoon olive oil
- 1 onion, finely chopped
- 2 carrots, diced
- 2 celery stalks, diced
- 3 cloves garlic, minced
- 1 teaspoon dried oregano
- 1 teaspoon dried thyme
- 1 bay leaf
- 1 pound boneless, skinless chicken breasts, cooked and shredded
- 1/2 cup orzo pasta
- 6 cups chicken broth
- Juice of 2 lemons
- Zest of 1 lemon
- Salt and black pepper to taste
- 1 cup baby spinach leaves
- 1/2 cup feta cheese, crumbled
- Fresh dill, chopped, for garnish
- Lemon slices, for garnish

Instructions:

In a large pot, heat olive oil over medium heat. Add the finely chopped onion, diced carrots, and diced celery. Cook until the vegetables are softened, about 5 minutes.

Add minced garlic, dried oregano, dried thyme, and the bay leaf. Stir well and cook for an additional 2 minutes until fragrant.

Pour in the chicken broth and bring the mixture to a simmer.

Stir in the shredded chicken and orzo pasta. Cook until the orzo is tender, following the package instructions.

Add the lemon juice and zest to the pot. Stir well to incorporate the lemon flavor.

Season the chowder with salt and black pepper to taste.

Just before serving, stir in the baby spinach leaves until wilted.

Ladle the Greek Lemon Chicken Chowder into bowls.

Garnish each bowl with crumbled feta cheese, chopped fresh dill, and lemon slices.

Serve hot and enjoy this bright and flavorful Greek Lemon Chicken Chowder!

This chowder combines the tanginess of lemon with the richness of chicken and orzo, creating a delightful Greek-inspired soup.

Curry Lentil Chowder

Ingredients:

- 1 tablespoon olive oil
- 1 onion, finely chopped
- 2 carrots, diced
- 2 celery stalks, diced
- 3 cloves garlic, minced
- 1 tablespoon curry powder
- 1 teaspoon ground cumin
- 1 teaspoon ground coriander
- 1 cup dried brown lentils, rinsed and drained
- 4 cups vegetable broth
- 1 can (14 ounces) diced tomatoes, undrained
- 1 can (14 ounces) coconut milk
- 1 sweet potato, peeled and diced
- Salt and black pepper to taste
- 1 cup baby spinach leaves
- Juice of 1 lime
- Fresh cilantro, chopped, for garnish
- Naan bread or rice, for serving

Instructions:

In a large pot, heat olive oil over medium heat. Add the finely chopped onion, diced carrots, and diced celery. Cook until the vegetables are softened, about 5 minutes.

Add minced garlic, curry powder, ground cumin, and ground coriander. Stir well and cook for an additional 2 minutes until fragrant.

Stir in the dried lentils, vegetable broth, diced tomatoes, coconut milk, and diced sweet potato. Bring the mixture to a boil.

Reduce the heat to low, cover the pot, and let it simmer for about 25-30 minutes, or until the lentils and sweet potatoes are tender.

Season the chowder with salt and black pepper to taste.

Just before serving, stir in the baby spinach leaves until wilted.

Squeeze the juice of one lime into the chowder and stir to combine.

Ladle the Curry Lentil Chowder into bowls.

Garnish each bowl with chopped fresh cilantro.
Serve hot with naan bread or over rice.
Enjoy this hearty and aromatic Curry Lentil Chowder!

This chowder combines the earthy flavors of lentils and sweet potatoes with the bold spices of curry, cumin, and coriander for a satisfying and delicious soup.

Jalapeño Popper Corn Chowder

Ingredients:

- 4 slices bacon, chopped
- 1 onion, finely chopped
- 2 cloves garlic, minced
- 2 jalapeños, seeds removed and finely chopped
- 1/4 cup all-purpose flour
- 4 cups chicken broth
- 3 cups frozen corn kernels
- 1 large potato, peeled and diced
- 2 cups milk
- 1 cup shredded cheddar cheese
- 1/2 cup cream cheese
- Salt and black pepper to taste
- Green onions, sliced, for garnish
- Jalapeño slices, for garnish
- Cornbread or crusty bread, for serving

Instructions:

In a large pot, cook the chopped bacon over medium heat until crispy. Remove bacon and set aside for garnish.
In the same pot, leave about 2 tablespoons of bacon fat and add the finely chopped onion, minced garlic, and chopped jalapeños. Cook until the vegetables are softened, about 5 minutes.
Stir in the all-purpose flour and cook for an additional 2 minutes to create a roux.
Pour in the chicken broth, stirring continuously to avoid lumps.
Add the frozen corn kernels and diced potato. Bring the mixture to a simmer and let it cook until the potatoes are tender, about 15-20 minutes.
Reduce the heat to low and stir in the milk.
Add the shredded cheddar cheese and cream cheese. Stir until the cheeses are melted and the chowder is creamy.
Season with salt and black pepper to taste.
Ladle the Jalapeño Popper Corn Chowder into bowls.
Garnish each bowl with crispy bacon, sliced green onions, and jalapeño slices.
Serve hot with cornbread or crusty bread.

Enjoy this spicy and cheesy Jalapeño Popper Corn Chowder!

This chowder combines the heat of jalapeños with the creaminess of cheddar and cream cheese, creating a flavorful and comforting soup.

Clam and Bacon Chowder

Ingredients:

- 4 slices bacon, chopped
- 1 onion, finely chopped
- 2 celery stalks, diced
- 2 cloves garlic, minced
- 1/4 cup all-purpose flour
- 4 cups clam juice
- 1 cup chicken broth
- 1 bay leaf
- 1/2 teaspoon dried thyme
- 1/4 teaspoon Old Bay seasoning (optional)
- 1 pound potatoes, peeled and diced
- 2 cups half-and-half
- 2 cans (10 ounces each) chopped clams, undrained
- Salt and black pepper to taste
- Fresh parsley, chopped, for garnish
- Oyster crackers, for serving

Instructions:

In a large pot, cook the chopped bacon over medium heat until crispy. Remove bacon and set aside for garnish.
In the same pot, leave about 2 tablespoons of bacon fat and add the finely chopped onion, diced celery, and minced garlic. Cook until the vegetables are softened, about 5 minutes.
Stir in the all-purpose flour and cook for an additional 2 minutes to create a roux.
Pour in the clam juice and chicken broth, stirring continuously to avoid lumps.
Add the bay leaf, dried thyme, Old Bay seasoning (if using), and diced potatoes. Bring the mixture to a simmer and let it cook until the potatoes are tender, about 15-20 minutes.
Reduce the heat to low and stir in the half-and-half.
Add the chopped clams with their juice. Simmer for an additional 5-10 minutes.
Season with salt and black pepper to taste.
Ladle the Clam and Bacon Chowder into bowls.
Garnish each bowl with crispy bacon and chopped fresh parsley.
Serve hot with oyster crackers on the side.

Enjoy this rich and flavorful Clam and Bacon Chowder!

This chowder combines the briny flavor of clams with the smokiness of bacon for a comforting and satisfying soup.

Creamy Asparagus and Ham Chowder

Ingredients:

- 2 tablespoons butter
- 1 onion, finely chopped
- 2 cloves garlic, minced
- 1/4 cup all-purpose flour
- 4 cups chicken broth
- 1 pound asparagus, trimmed and cut into bite-sized pieces
- 1 cup diced ham
- 1 cup potatoes, peeled and diced
- 1 bay leaf
- 1 teaspoon dried thyme
- Salt and black pepper to taste
- 2 cups half-and-half
- 1 cup shredded cheddar cheese
- Fresh parsley, chopped, for garnish

Instructions:

In a large pot, melt the butter over medium heat. Add the finely chopped onion and cook until softened, about 5 minutes.
Add minced garlic and cook for an additional 1-2 minutes until fragrant.
Stir in the all-purpose flour to create a roux. Cook for 2-3 minutes, stirring constantly.
Gradually pour in the chicken broth, stirring continuously to avoid lumps.
Add the asparagus, diced ham, diced potatoes, bay leaf, and dried thyme. Bring the mixture to a simmer and let it cook until the vegetables are tender, about 15-20 minutes.
Season with salt and black pepper to taste.
Reduce the heat to low and stir in the half-and-half. Simmer for an additional 5-10 minutes.
Add the shredded cheddar cheese and stir until melted.
Remove the bay leaf from the pot.
Ladle the Creamy Asparagus and Ham Chowder into bowls.
Garnish each bowl with chopped fresh parsley.
Serve hot and enjoy this comforting Creamy Asparagus and Ham Chowder!

This chowder combines the freshness of asparagus with the savory flavor of ham and the creaminess of cheddar for a delightful and satisfying soup.

Spinach and White Bean Chowder

Ingredients:

- 2 tablespoons olive oil
- 1 onion, finely chopped
- 2 carrots, diced
- 2 celery stalks, diced
- 3 cloves garlic, minced
- 1 teaspoon dried thyme
- 1 teaspoon dried rosemary
- 1 bay leaf
- 4 cups vegetable broth
- 2 cans (15 ounces each) white beans, drained and rinsed
- 1 pound potatoes, peeled and diced
- 4 cups fresh spinach leaves, chopped
- Salt and black pepper to taste
- 1 cup milk
- 1 cup half-and-half
- 1/2 cup grated Parmesan cheese
- Fresh parsley, chopped, for garnish

Instructions:

In a large pot, heat olive oil over medium heat. Add the finely chopped onion, diced carrots, and diced celery. Cook until the vegetables are softened, about 5 minutes.

Add minced garlic, dried thyme, dried rosemary, and the bay leaf. Stir well and cook for an additional 2 minutes until fragrant.

Pour in the vegetable broth and bring the mixture to a simmer.

Add the drained and rinsed white beans, diced potatoes, and chopped spinach.

Simmer until the potatoes are tender, about 15-20 minutes.

Season the chowder with salt and black pepper to taste.

Reduce the heat to low and stir in the milk and half-and-half.

Add grated Parmesan cheese and stir until melted.

Remove the bay leaf from the pot.

Ladle the Spinach and White Bean Chowder into bowls.

Garnish each bowl with chopped fresh parsley.

Serve hot and enjoy this nutritious and flavorful Spinach and White Bean Chowder!

This chowder combines the heartiness of white beans and potatoes with the vibrant green color and nutrients of fresh spinach for a wholesome and tasty soup.

Chicken and Poblano Chowder

Ingredients:

- 2 poblano peppers
- 2 tablespoons olive oil
- 1 onion, finely chopped
- 2 cloves garlic, minced
- 1 teaspoon ground cumin
- 1 teaspoon chili powder
- 1/2 teaspoon smoked paprika
- 1/4 cup all-purpose flour
- 4 cups chicken broth
- 1 pound boneless, skinless chicken breasts, cooked and shredded
- 2 cups corn kernels (fresh or frozen)
- 1 cup diced potatoes
- 1 cup diced carrots
- 1 cup diced celery
- Salt and black pepper to taste
- 2 cups milk
- 1 cup half-and-half
- 1 cup shredded Monterey Jack cheese
- Fresh cilantro, chopped, for garnish
- Lime wedges, for serving

Instructions:

Preheat the broiler. Place poblano peppers on a baking sheet and broil, turning occasionally, until the skin is blistered and charred. Transfer the peppers to a bowl, cover with plastic wrap, and let them steam for about 10 minutes. Peel off the skins, remove seeds, and chop the peppers.
In a large pot, heat olive oil over medium heat. Add the finely chopped onion and cook until softened, about 5 minutes.
Add minced garlic, ground cumin, chili powder, and smoked paprika. Stir well and cook for an additional 2 minutes until fragrant.
Stir in the all-purpose flour to create a roux. Cook for 2-3 minutes, stirring constantly.
Pour in the chicken broth, stirring continuously to avoid lumps.

Add shredded chicken, corn kernels, diced potatoes, diced carrots, diced celery, chopped poblano peppers, salt, and black pepper. Bring the mixture to a simmer and let it cook until the vegetables are tender, about 15-20 minutes.
Reduce the heat to low and stir in the milk and half-and-half.
Add shredded Monterey Jack cheese and stir until melted.
Adjust the seasoning if needed.
Ladle the Chicken and Poblano Chowder into bowls.
Garnish each bowl with chopped fresh cilantro.
Serve hot with lime wedges on the side.
Enjoy this delicious and mildly spicy Chicken and Poblano Chowder!

This chowder combines the smoky flavor of poblano peppers with the richness of shredded chicken and a creamy broth for a comforting and satisfying soup.

Apple and Cheddar Chowder

Ingredients:

- 3 tablespoons unsalted butter
- 1 onion, finely chopped
- 2 carrots, diced
- 2 celery stalks, diced
- 2 Granny Smith apples, peeled, cored, and diced
- 3 tablespoons all-purpose flour
- 4 cups chicken broth
- 2 cups milk
- 1 cup half-and-half
- 3 cups diced potatoes
- Salt and black pepper to taste
- 2 cups sharp cheddar cheese, shredded
- 1/2 cup sour cream
- Chives, chopped, for garnish

Instructions:

In a large pot, melt the butter over medium heat. Add the finely chopped onion, diced carrots, diced celery, and diced apples. Cook until the vegetables are softened, about 5 minutes.
Stir in the all-purpose flour to create a roux. Cook for 2-3 minutes, stirring constantly.
Gradually pour in the chicken broth, stirring continuously to avoid lumps.
Add the milk and half-and-half. Stir well to combine.
Add diced potatoes, salt, and black pepper. Bring the mixture to a simmer and let it cook until the potatoes are tender, about 15-20 minutes.
Reduce the heat to low and stir in the shredded sharp cheddar cheese until melted.
Stir in the sour cream, ensuring it is well incorporated.
Adjust the seasoning if needed.
Ladle the Apple and Cheddar Chowder into bowls.
Garnish each bowl with chopped chives.
Serve hot and enjoy this unique and comforting Apple and Cheddar Chowder!

This chowder combines the sweetness of apples with the savory richness of cheddar cheese for a delicious twist on the classic chowder.

Smoked Salmon Chowder

Ingredients:

- 2 tablespoons unsalted butter
- 1 onion, finely chopped
- 2 celery stalks, diced
- 2 carrots, diced
- 2 cloves garlic, minced
- 1/4 cup all-purpose flour
- 4 cups fish or vegetable broth
- 1 cup half-and-half
- 1 cup milk
- 3 cups potatoes, peeled and diced
- 8 ounces smoked salmon, flaked
- 1 teaspoon dried dill
- Salt and black pepper to taste
- 1 cup frozen corn kernels
- 1/2 cup sour cream
- Chives, chopped, for garnish

Instructions:

In a large pot, melt the butter over medium heat. Add the finely chopped onion, diced celery, diced carrots, and minced garlic. Cook until the vegetables are softened, about 5 minutes.
Stir in the all-purpose flour to create a roux. Cook for 2-3 minutes, stirring constantly.
Gradually pour in the fish or vegetable broth, stirring continuously to avoid lumps.
Add the half-and-half and milk. Stir well to combine.
Add diced potatoes, flaked smoked salmon, dried dill, salt, and black pepper.
Bring the mixture to a simmer and let it cook until the potatoes are tender, about 15-20 minutes.
Reduce the heat to low and stir in the frozen corn kernels.
Just before serving, stir in the sour cream, ensuring it is well incorporated.
Adjust the seasoning if needed.
Ladle the Smoked Salmon Chowder into bowls.
Garnish each bowl with chopped chives.
Serve hot and enjoy this rich and flavorful Smoked Salmon Chowder!

This chowder features the distinct flavor of smoked salmon, creating a creamy and comforting soup with a touch of dill for added freshness.

Ham and Potato Chowder

Ingredients:

- 3 tablespoons unsalted butter
- 1 onion, finely chopped
- 2 carrots, diced
- 2 celery stalks, diced
- 3 cloves garlic, minced
- 1/4 cup all-purpose flour
- 4 cups chicken broth
- 3 cups potatoes, peeled and diced
- 2 cups cooked ham, diced
- 1 teaspoon dried thyme
- Salt and black pepper to taste
- 2 cups milk
- 1 cup half-and-half
- 1 cup sharp cheddar cheese, shredded
- Green onions, sliced, for garnish

Instructions:

In a large pot, melt the butter over medium heat. Add the finely chopped onion, diced carrots, diced celery, and minced garlic. Cook until the vegetables are softened, about 5 minutes.

Stir in the all-purpose flour to create a roux. Cook for 2-3 minutes, stirring constantly.

Gradually pour in the chicken broth, stirring continuously to avoid lumps.

Add diced potatoes, diced ham, dried thyme, salt, and black pepper. Bring the mixture to a simmer and let it cook until the potatoes are tender, about 15-20 minutes.

Reduce the heat to low and stir in the milk and half-and-half.

Add shredded sharp cheddar cheese and stir until melted.

Adjust the seasoning if needed.

Ladle the Ham and Potato Chowder into bowls.

Garnish each bowl with sliced green onions.

Serve hot and enjoy this hearty and comforting Ham and Potato Chowder!

This chowder combines the savory flavor of ham with tender potatoes and a creamy broth, creating a satisfying and delicious soup.

Creamy Cauliflower Chowder

Ingredients:

- 2 tablespoons olive oil
- 1 onion, finely chopped
- 2 carrots, diced
- 2 celery stalks, diced
- 3 cloves garlic, minced
- 1 head cauliflower, chopped into florets
- 1/4 cup all-purpose flour
- 4 cups vegetable broth
- 2 cups milk
- 1 cup half-and-half
- 1 teaspoon dried thyme
- Salt and black pepper to taste
- 1 cup shredded sharp cheddar cheese
- 1/2 cup grated Parmesan cheese
- Fresh parsley, chopped, for garnish

Instructions:

In a large pot, heat olive oil over medium heat. Add the finely chopped onion, diced carrots, diced celery, and minced garlic. Cook until the vegetables are softened, about 5 minutes.
Add the cauliflower florets and cook for an additional 5 minutes.
Stir in the all-purpose flour to create a roux. Cook for 2-3 minutes, stirring constantly.
Gradually pour in the vegetable broth, stirring continuously to avoid lumps.
Add the milk, half-and-half, dried thyme, salt, and black pepper. Bring the mixture to a simmer and let it cook until the cauliflower is tender, about 15-20 minutes.
Reduce the heat to low and stir in the shredded sharp cheddar cheese and grated Parmesan cheese until melted.
Adjust the seasoning if needed.
Using an immersion blender, blend the chowder to your desired consistency. You can leave it slightly chunky or blend it until smooth.
Ladle the Creamy Cauliflower Chowder into bowls.
Garnish each bowl with chopped fresh parsley.
Serve hot and enjoy this creamy and comforting Cauliflower Chowder!

This chowder is a wholesome and nutritious option, replacing traditional potatoes with cauliflower for a velvety texture and rich flavor.

www.ingramcontent.com/pod-product-compliance
Lightning Source LLC
LaVergne TN
LVHW081612060526
838201LV00054B/2223